Dedication

"To All Children with Special Needs in the World."

-Syeda Khanom, PH.D

Special Baby: Special Needs - 1

Syeda Khanom, Ph.D

ASA PUBLISHING CORPORATION
AN INNOVATIVE OUTSOURCE BOOK PUBLISHING HYBRID

Copyrights©2024, Syeda Khanom Ph.D, All Rights Reserved
Book Title: Special Baby: Special Needs - 1
Date Published: 02.27.2024
Book ID: ASAPCID2380900
Edition: 1 *Trade Paperback*
ISBN: 978-1-960104-42-7
Library of Congress Cataloging-in-Publication Data

This book was published in the United States of America.
Great State of Michigan

Table of Contents

Introduction

Many children around us in our family, relatives, or acquaintances have long-term physical or mental disabilities or both. These psychophysical complications, or a specific learning disability (in speaking, reading, writing, counting, and cognition problems) make the child unable to demonstrate his age-appropriate behaviors and ability to perform daily tasks like his peers. These babies are called special babies or children with special needs. For example, children with Autism, Dyslexia, Dyspraxia, Dysgraphia, Developmental Delay, Dyscalculia, Cerebral Palsy, Down syndrome, and any other special needs.

To develop the learning process of these special children and to nourish or improve their latent talents, when a special education protocol (special education materials, additional teacher recruitment, training, etc.) is arranged inclusively or additionally or separately from ordinary children, it is called *special education needs* (Children and Families Act, 2014, Section: 20; Marks, 2000; SEND Code of Practice, 2014; Khan and Mohammad, 2011; Ackerman et al., 2005). Interestingly, there are currently at least 93 million children with special needs around the world (UNICEF, 2017).

In Bangladesh, there are about 18 million children with special needs, ranging in age from 6 to 11 years. Only 1-2% of them have the right to receive special education, and girls are relatively less entitled to it (Ackerman et al., 2005). Overall, there are few educational opportunities for special children in Bangladesh, so parents and teachers must face many difficulties in identifying the perceived needs of children with special needs.

However, the special needs of every child are a human condition with unique characteristics (WHO, 2011). This human condition can be identified in due procedure according to the specific characteristics and nature associated with it, and specific education can be imparted precisely. As a result, the latent talents of children can be cultivated, and the lives of these children can be made creative and promising (Ibid., 2011).

Offering children the fundamental right to education in light of their unique special needs is now an internationally recognized propaganda. The rights of children to special needs education have also been considered an international notification for the last few decades by the initiatives of the Salamanca Statement (1994), the universal pioneer of international education policy. Bangladesh has expressed a cooperative opinion in this regard.

Countries around the world and international organizations have been working together for decades to implement this pledge of the Salamanca Statement (1994:1) "education for all" to establish the fundamental right of children with special needs to education. However, the Salamanca Statement not only considers the special needs of children as an inclusive learning activity or strategy, but also proposes action plans to establish children's fundamental right to education according to their unique characteristics, nature, needs, and perceived learning strategies (Lindsay, 2003).

As a result, children with special needs have been allocated the right to be automatically included in any educational institution, including mainstream educational institutions worldwide. Most significantly, the Salamanca Statement has made well-known international proposals and recommendations to establish the right of children with special needs to positive participation and inclusion in inclusive education in any educational institution (The Salamanca Statement, 1994).

Nearly two decades ago, Bangladesh also expressed solidarity with one of the signatory countries for the proposals and recommendations of this international education policy aimed at establishing the right to education for children with special needs (Ackerman et al., 2005). As a result, national education policy and legislation (Bangladesh Persons with Disability Welfare Act, 2001; The National Education Policy, 2010) have been formulated as a continuous step. The main objective of this is to recognize the right of any physically and mentally disabled child to participate in any educational activity in any educational institution in light of its learning strategy, type, nature, and characteristics.

Subsequently, under the Disability Rights and Protection Act, 2013, to further establish the legal and social rights of children, legal definitions and features have been provided for some special needs, including autism, cerebral palsy, and Down Syndrome, which play an effective role in identifying children with special needs. However, as there is no specific guideline in the law regarding the methods and learning strategies for identifying these special needs, there is a complexity in organizing, cooperating, and providing special education in the family environment and in educational institutions for the proper development of the learning process for these children with special needs.

Moreover, under the National Education Policy (2010) and Disability Rights and Protection Act (2013), there are no specific guidelines or outlines regarding specific learning disabilities of the special needs of the child: dyslexia, developmental delay, so it is not possible for parents and teachers to properly identify the child with these needs. As a result, the educational lives of these children remain risky. However, in the practical implementation of national education policy and legislation, Bangladesh is administering special education programs in various private schools and institutions, including thirteen government schools (Ackerman et al., 2005). The main objective of these programs is to establish the fundamental right of children with special needs to participate in educational activities in any educational setting. Still, a very limited number of children with special needs have the opportunity to receive education in these institutions. However, it is vital to identify children easily and accurately with special needs across the country. Therefore, considering the importance of applying proper learning strategies through decent identification of children with special needs, this book focuses on the characteristics, symptoms, causes, identification methods, and learning strategies of Autism, Dyslexia, Dyspraxia, Dysgraphia, Dyscalculia, Developmental Delay, Cerebral Palsy, and Down Syndrome (Chapters 1-8).

Practical examples (Chapter 9) of these special needs are also provided. In this way, parents, authorities, and teachers of the respective educational institutions, social workers, policymakers, other professionals, and the general public can get a basic idea about the special needs of a particular child and become aware of the appropriate learning needs of these children. At the same time, they will be able to play an active role in achieving the goals of national and international education policies to establish the fundamental right of these children to education. This is because knowing the characteristics, symptoms, causes, identification methods, and learning strategies of a particular child's special needs will make it possible to organize a suitable special education system for them. As a result, their basic right to education will be socially established. And by getting the basic idea and getting the overall direction regarding the special needs of the child, the teachers, parents, and others will be able to identify the special needs correctly and help the children develop the appropriate learning process.

References

Ackerman, P., et al., (2005). *Assessment of educational needs of disabled children in Bangladesh.* United States Agency of International Development (USAID).

Bangladesh Persons with Disability Welfare Act. (2001). Dhaka: National Forum of Organization Working with Disabled (NFOWD).

Khan, N., & Mohammed, A. (2001). The status of unserved children in education. *Children with disability in Bangladesh. A situation analysis.* Dhaka: CAMPE (Campaign of Popular Education).

Lindsay, B. (2003). What future for special schools and inclusion? Conceptual and professional perspectives. Guildford Lecture. *British Journal of Special Education, 30(1), 3-10.*

Marks, J. (2000). *What Are Special Education Needs? An analysis of new growth industry.* Centre for Policy Studies. London: The Chameleon Press.

National Education Policy. (2010). Ministry of Education. The Government of the People's Republic of Bangladesh.

The Children and Families Act, Section 20. (2014).

> https://www.legislations.gov.UK.government/publicatio
> ns

The Salamanca Statement. On Principle, Policy, and Practice in Special Needs Education. (1994). *United Nations Educational, Scientific and Cultural Organization (UNESCO).* Spain: Salamanca.

The Special Education Needs and Disability (SEND) Code of Practice. (2014).

> SEND code of practice: 0 to 25 years - GOV.UK
> (www.gov.uk)

The United Nations Children Fund (UNICEF). 2017. Disabilities: Introduction.

> https://www.unicef.org/disabilities/introduction.

World Health Organization. (2011). World Report on Disability.

> World Report on Disability (who.int)

Persons with Disabilities Rights and Protection Act, 2013, Section 4. Department of Law and Secretariat, Ministry of Law and Judiciary Government of the People's Republic of Bangladesh, Dhaka, Bangladesh.

Special Baby:
Special Needs - 1

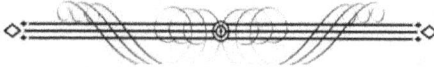

Syeda Khanom, Ph.D

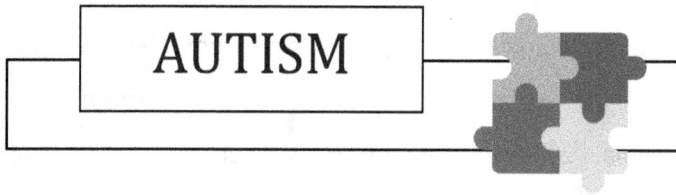

AUTISM

CHAPTER 1

Autism: Difficulty in Developing Social Skills

Autism is a neurodevelopmental disorder that affects children from birth and lasts a lifetime (American Psychiatric Association, 2013). Difficulties in developing innate social skills can be observed in children with autism. This is called the Triad of Impairment because children have weaknesses in achieving social communication skills, social interaction skills, and difficulty displaying imaginative behavior (Bowler, 2007; American Psychiatric Association, 2013). Originally, autism is a Greek word derived from the suffix 'aut' (meaning 'self'), and 'ism' (meaning 'state'). So, semantically autism means "stay in the self" (Wire, 2005).

In 1911, a Swiss psychiatrist named Eugen Bleuler was the first to use the term autism to describe a special feature of schizophrenia (Bowler, 2007). According to him, people with autism seem to be living in a different world. The characteristic he explained was later described in two separate research papers by Child Specialist, Leo Kanner in 1943, respectively, as *Autistic Disturbances of Affective Contact*, and in 1944, Austrian

Physician, Asperger called it *Autistic Psychopathy*. They argued that people with autism are largely isolated from others because of a lack of social communication and interaction skills (Bogdashina, 2000). Later on, researchers suggested that children with autism may also have difficulty reflecting repetitive and imaginative behaviors (Ibid., 2000; Autism Speak, n.d.).

Characteristics and Symptoms

The following features and symptoms (Bowler, 2007; American Psychiatric Association, 2013; Bogdashina, 2000) are most commonly observed in children with autism:

- Neurological complex developmental impairment, which is observed between 6 months and 3 years of age. In this case, psychophysical development, and gross and fine motor development are very slow (learning to lift the neck late, sitting up late, learning to crawl late, having difficulty or delay in eating, chewing, and biting food).

- Problems establishing verbal and non-verbal communication, for example: the child cannot establish social communication by eye contact; delay to hold a pen or bubbling; speech delay (speaking after 14 months) or not be able to speak or use limited words; The child may not able to point out by the finger or ask for something, but may be able to do so by pulling the other person's hand or gesturing; The baby does not respond when called by his name (within twelve months); The child cannot imitate other or can't stand in front of a mirror to imitate himself; He does not understand how to wave hands, but wave his hands upside down.

- Limitations on maintaining social and reciprocal interaction: Being alone in one's own world, that is, not being able to interact with one's peers or others, or having problems interacting; Not being able to make friends or maintain friendships; children are reluctant to play with peers; The child's emotions are very low; The child may not understand the usual courtesy of shaking hands, smiling as they meet, or hugging others, not even hugging their parents, or not noticing their absence.

- Having trouble performing imaginative behaviors: imaginative games, such as a child cannot play with his hands like an airplane (unless within 18 months); can't tell a story; and play with Exceptional objects such as key rings, bottles, and bottle-lids, lids of any cooking utensils and mobiles. There are limitations in the development of cognitive or thinking skills.

- Having difficulty in performing stereotype or repetitive behaviors (repetitive behavior means constantly saying the same words or doing the same task): repeatedly opening and closing the door of the house or the door of the fridge; The child walks with pressure on thumb or toe; repeatedly biting his hand and repeatedly touching the tongue with his hand inside the mouth.

- Exhibiting tic disorder: Then the screaming incessantly in a hoarse voice; tweaking others; pulling other's hair; hitting the ground with the head; echolalia (means to say the same word over and over again like a parrot), being more or less sensitive to hearing, sight, touch, smell, taste, pain, balance, and movement.

- Children may have intellectual disabilities or seizures.

- Crying with excessive agitation, excitement, or inconsistency and feeling restless in the noise around.

- Children tend to follow the same routine or become too stubborn; they may have extraordinary skills in any specific or exceptional subject.

- The developmental learning process of a child with autism is usually faster than that of a child with delayed development.

Causes

The exact cause of autism is not yet known. However, genetic and environmental factors (Morton & Firth, 1995; Ratajczak,

2001; Autism Speaks, n.d.) can increase the risk of autism in a child.

A. Genetic causes

- About one hundred genes have been identified in autism. These include NKGN3, NLGN4, NRXN1, MecP2, HOXA1, DbtaH, Fraxile-x, FMR-1, Reelin, SHANK2, and others. If there are any changes or deficiencies, or mutations that occur in these genes, they increase a child's risk of developing autism.

- If someone else in the family, such as parents or older siblings, has autism, the next child may also have autism. Brain immaturity can be seen in children with autism. Usually, the frontal lobe of the brain is responsible for socialization and speech, perception, or thinking processes. As the frontal lobe of a child with autism becomes immature, the child's cognitive development is hampered or slowed down.

B. Environmental causes

- If a child has any other specific disorder or learning disability that impairs the development and function of the brain, the child's risk of developing autism is greatly increased. Often, a child with autism has co-occurring other psycho-physical problems such as dyslexia, dyspraxia, depression, frustration, bipolar disorder, schizophrenia, Tourette syndrome, Down syndrome, seizures, pica, Type 1 diabetes, hypothyroidism, hypertension, tuberculosis, metabolic problem, fragile-x syndrome, Rett Syndrome, gastric, infection in the nose, ear and neck, inattention and restlessness, ADHD, Angelman Syndrome, and any other health problem.

- If the mother has uncontrolled diabetes during pregnancy.
- If there are any inborn problems (premature birth or jaundice).
- If the father is older and the mother is over 30 years old.
- According to many researchers, some vaccines can cause autism in children.

Types

There are three main types of autism in terms of the presence of the three main features and symptoms (social communication, social interaction, and imaginative behaviors) of autism in children (American Psychiatric Association, 2013; Autism Support for West Shore, 2014; Autism, n.d.).

a. Classical Autism

- The level of presence of the three main symptoms of

autism in a child with classical autism is very acute. Symptoms of autism are most common in children between the ages of 6 months and 3 years. These include:

- Children learn to lift their necks late, sit up late, crawl late, and walk late. The child may or may not be able to bubble, or it is too late and limited. The child can't speak at all or utter very limited words.

- The level of annoying and repetitive behavior in a child is very high, especially echolalia, sudden laughter, and sudden crying.

- The child sleeps very little at night or has trouble sleeping and suddenly wakes up and cries incessantly.

- The child does not respond at all to being called by name or jingling. Children do not play with toys at all with peers; most of the time, they stay alone or isolated from others.

- The child does not have the ability to establish new relationships, maintain relationships with peers, or socialize with others.

- The child cannot imitate others or imitate themselves in the mirror at all.

- The child cannot blow on food, blow out candles, or blow on bubbles.

- The child has very little understanding of emotion and courtesy (shaking hands, waving hands, hugging).
- The child usually has an intellectual disability and seizures.
- Children may not play imaginative, creative, and constructive games at all.
- Children develop hypersensitivity to the sound of doors, water, cars, combing hair, brushing their teeth, and touching others.
- It is very difficult for a child to move through the use of fine and gross motors or to maintain balance in the eyes, hands, legs, and other parts of the body.
- The child cannot show anything by pointing his fingers.

b. High-functioning Autism or Asperger's Syndrome

Typically, in this type, the three main symptoms of autism in a child are not as severe as in classical autism, and the symptoms appear within one and a half to three years. These include:

- Usually, the child does not have an intellectual disability, or even if it does, it is limited.
- Usually, children learn to speak in a timely manner, but find it difficult to communicate with others through normal conversation.
- Children cannot convey their opinions, likes, and dislikes

to others while some talk irrelevantly and repeat excessively and ask the same question over and over again. Some, on the other hand, speak very little or are not interested in talking.

- The child has difficulty interacting with peers or others.
- Moreover, children are stubborn and monotonous.

Scientist Albert Einstein is thought to have had Asperger's syndrome.

C. Pervasive Developmental Disorder

These children usually have symptoms of autism, but their levels are relatively lower than the above two types and have some similarities and differences from the other two.

For example:

- Other problems with autism gradually decrease after a child learns to speak.
- Intellectual disabilities may or may not exist in the child.

Autistic Savant

Some children with autism possess special skills (such as math, sports, arts, music, acting, computers, or any other field); they are called autistic savants. Dustin Hoffman, in the Hollywood movie RAIN MAN, and Shah Rukh Khan, in the

Bollywood movie MY NAME IS KHAN, played the role of Autistic Savant.

Diagnosis Methods

- So far, no specific scientific reliance on autism detection has been developed. However, the difference between white and gray matter in the brain of a child through Magnetic Resonance Imaging (MRI) or Computed Tomography Scan (CT scan) can be detected, a neurologist can examine that to find out if the child has autism.

- According to the DSM-IV guidelines (American Psychiatric Association, 2013), a child can be considered to have autism if he or she has any of the six characteristics of autism.

Learning Techniques

Autism cannot be completely eradicated, but with proper learning strategies, a child's learning and developmental skills can be improved. However, it is not possible to reduce the symptoms of autism by applying only one strategy (Jordan, 2008). The following strategies (Gray, 2004; Mannix, 1998; Potter & Whittaker, 2001; Rosenwasser et al., 2001; Macintyre, 2002; Jordan, 2008; Kouijzer et al., 2009; Delaney, T. OTR, 2010) can be applied to the development of the autistic child's learning process according to the child's age and needs:

- Medication: Apply vitamins and drugs that enhance brain function. Taking medication to reduce depression, anxiety, and restlessness.
- Applied behavior analysis.
- Picture Exchange Communication System and Social Skill Training Program.
- Storytelling and social stories.
- Play activities. However, the use of colorful toys in sports positively develops the child's cognitive development.
- Information and communication technology.
- Speech therapy.
- Neurofeedback, neuromodulation, Neuro Muscular Electrical Stimulator, Transcutaneous Electrical Nerve Stimulation (TENSE).
- Behavior Modification Strategy.
- Cognitive Behavior Therapy.
- Psychodynamic approach.

Applying precise and proper strategies at the right time and at a young age can greatly reduce a child's autism levels and positively change his social skills, perceptions, and behavior.

References

American Psychiatric Association. (2013). *The Diagnostic and Statistical Manual of Mental Disorder*. 5th ed. Washington, DC: American Psychiatric Association.

Autism Speaks. (n.d.). *Autism risk and maternal diabetes with obesity: What you need to know?* www.autismspeaks.org/search?search_api_fulltext=diabetes+with+obesity

Autism Support of West Shore. (2014). *What is Autism?* www.asws.org/what-is-autism

Bogdashina, O. (2006). *Theory of Mind and Triad of Perspectives on Autism and Asperger Syndrome. A view from the Bridge*. London: Jessica Kingsley's Publications.

Bowler, D. M. (2007). *Autistic Spectrum Disorders: psychological theory and research*. Sussex: John Willey & Son's LTD.

Delaney, T., & OTR, M. S. (2010). *101 Games and Activities for Children with Autism, Asperger's, and Sensory Processing Disorders*. London: McGraw Hill.

Gray, C. (1994). *The Social Story Books*. Arlington, TX: Future Horizons.

Hupfeld, K. E., & Ketcham, C. J. (2016). Behavioral effects of transcranial direct current stimulation on motor and language planning in minimally verbal children with autism spectrum disorder: Feasibility, limitations, and future directions. *Journal of Childhood & Developmental Disorders*, 2(3), 1-10.

Jordan, R. (2008). Autistic Spectrum Disorders: a challenge and model for inclusion in education. *British Journal of Special Education,* 35(1), 11-15.

Kouijzer, M. E. J. et al., (2009). Neurofeedback treatment in autism. Preliminary findings in behavioral, cognitive, and neurophysiological functioning. *Research in Autism Spectrum Disorders.* doi: 10.1016/j.rasd.2009.10.007. G model. RASD-216. 1. 14.

Macintyre, C. (2002). *Play for Children with Special Needs.* London: David Fulton Publishers.

Mannix, D. (1998). *Social Skills Activities for Secondary Students with Special Education Needs.* San Francisco, CA: Jossey-Bass.

Morton, J., & Frith, U. (1995). Causal modeling: Structural approaches to developmental psychopathology. In D. Cicchetti & D. Cohen. (Eds.). *Developmental Psychopathology*, 357-390. New York, NY: Wiley.

Potter, C., & Whittaker, C. (2001). *Enabling Communication in Children with Autism.* London: Jessica Kingsley

Publications.

Ratajczak, V. H. (2001). Theoretical aspects of autism cause

a review. *Journal of Immunotoxicology, 8(1),* 68-79.

Rosenwasser et al., (2001). (Ed.). Autism Part 1. *Behavior*

Modification, 25(5), 671-802.

Persons with Disabilities Rights and Protection Act, 2013, Section

4. Department of Law and Secretariat, Ministry of Law and

Judiciary Government of the People's Republic of Bangladesh,

Dhaka, Bangladesh.

DYSLEXIA

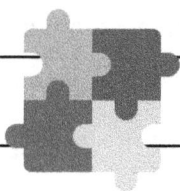

CHAPTER 2
Dyslexia: Reading Difficulty

Dyslexia *is not a disorder, but a disability. Dyslexia is a special form of learning disability that impairs a child's ability to read and spell something spontaneously and clearly, or appropriately, and impedes the development and expression of language skills (The Rose Report, 2009; Waller et al., 2000; Armstrong & Humphrey, 2006). To put it more clearly, it is called dyslexia when a child, despite having normal intelligence and abilities, finds it difficult to pronounce words or sounds or letters and has difficulty reading or spelling words or sounds, and writing words (Cheever, 2001:1).*

The term dyslexia originate from the Greek word "dys", which means "difficulty", and "lexis", which means words. Thus, dyslexia are a problem "with reading words". (Ibid., 2001). Usually, part of the occipital lobe of the brain is associated with learning to read, and when it encounters an impediment to the communication of pictorial or written symbols, the child has difficulty reading (Avlidou, 2015; Shywiz, 1996). Regardless, dyslexia is not thoroughly associated with brain injury or accident or parental incompetence (Shashtry, 2007 cited in Williams & Lynch, 2010).

The term dyslexia was first used in 1887 when it was described as an inborn "word blindness". It was later considered difficult to read precisely until the 1920s, and the term was used to refer to a variety of learning disabilities (The Rose Report, 2009). The term dyslexia is currently used to describe more than 70 different types of learning disabilities, so it is called the mother of learning disabilities (Davis & Braun, 1994).

Dyslexia, as a specific learning disability, is related to the unequal balance of learning skills, which has a neurological basis. It is associated with structural and functional traits, differences, or difficulties of the brain (The National Centre for Learning Disability, 2014; Lucid Research, 2006).

Many of the world's most famous celebrities, including Tom Cruise, Steven Spielberg, Albert Einstein, Leonardo da Vinci, Abhishek Bachchan, and many more are known to have dyslexia.

Characteristics

Children with dyslexia have an imbalance or weaknesses in achieving learning skills, usually in the following cases (Shyrwiz, 1996; The British Dyslexia Association, 2007; The Rose Report, 2009; Williams & Lynch, 2010; National Centre for Learning

Disabilities, 2014; Avlidou, 2015; Nordqvist, 2016):

a. Having difficulty processing verbal and written language information or acquiring linguistic skills through sounds or words.

b. Many find it difficult to process information related to verbal memory and processing.

c. Difficulty in performing or coordinating the movement of gross and fine motors, and the difficulty in proper application of the left or right-hand combination, or mixed use. The processing of sound or phonological information is usually observed in children with dyslexia. In children, imbalance or inconsistency may arise in using of working memory and coordinating gross and fine motor skills and developing automatic learning skills with other perceptual or cognitive learning skills, which makes it difficult for him to complete the literacy stage. It also has a negative impact on the child's acquisition of formal learning skills and psychosocial development.

d. Dyslexia is more common in boys than in girls, with a ratio of 1:4. However, some coexistence prevails with the development, weakness in expression and acquisition of language skills, motor coordination difficulty, mental developmental difficulties, inattention and extreme instability, personal incompatibility, social communication problems, and many other psychosocial and physical problems. However, they are not due to individual reasons, but due to dyslexia.

Symptoms

Symptoms of dyslexia (Chievers, 2001; Waller et al., 2000; Davis & Braun, 1994; Williams & Lynch, 2010; The Rose Report, 2009; Lucid Research, 2006; Nordqvist, 2016; The National Centre for Learning Disabilities, 2014; Shywiz, 1996; The British Dyslexia Association, 2007; Snowling, 2000; Snowling, 2012) in children begin in pre-early childhood and persist into adulthood, as discussed below:

a. **Preschool Period**
- Children have speech delays or difficulty speaking.
- The child has difficulty articulating expressive language and has weakness in the application of oral, speech, and written forms of language.
- Children find it difficult to recite rhymes.
- The child is less interested in learning the alphabet and has difficulty learning.
- Children cannot sort letters alphabetically.

- The use of the left hand and the right hand is contradictory and makes many mistakes.
- The child pays very little attention to learning.
- Fine motor coordination or circulation skills are very weak in children.

b. Primary School Period

- The child lacks the knowledge and skills to recognize letters and sounds or phonics, or to distinguish between them.
- Difficulty in understanding phonological awareness means that there is a problem with the relationship of letters to sounds and coordination when pronouncing letters.
- There are problems learning, mastering, and remembering the alphabet.
- Spell something very whimsically.
- Children find it difficult to read and write from texts.
- Children find it difficult to copy anything from the school board.
- The child's handwriting is vague or scribbled in nature.
- The child has difficulty in reciting rhymes.
- Children find it difficult to use and apply sounds and

words appropriately and have difficulty adding, deducting, and revising syllables.

- Children have difficulty pronouncing shattered words, applying words, and adding new words.
- The child has problems with the movement and coordination of fine and gross motors and gestures.
- Children have difficulty in expressing short-term memory skills.
- When three or more instructions are given to the child, he or she can follow only one instruction.

c. **Middle School Period**

- Children find it difficult to pronounce words and sounds and to perceive their structural differences.
- The child's reading speed is very slow in nature.
- When a child hears a new or unfamiliar word, he or she feels weak in remembering and understanding the meaning.
- The child may have difficulty spelling phonetic and non-phonetic sounds.
- Children find it difficult to decipher age-appropriate reading and writing.
- Children find it difficult to learn foreign languages.
- The child has difficulty recognizing words or phrases

while reading.

- The child has difficulty understanding and interpreting the text or content.

- Children have difficulty coordinating pronunciation to words.

- The child may have difficulty coordinating and performing word pronunciation with gestures.

- The child misspells oral and written spellings.

- Children cannot distinguish between letters or words that sound similar, such as 'b and d', 'p and q', '6 and 9', 'bed and bad', 'sea and see', and others.

- Lack of self-awareness.

d. Adulthood

- Having difficulty reading and writing.

- The writing speed was very slow.

- There are weaknesses in performing organizational and expressive tasks.

- Lack of self-awareness.

If the child shows the above symptoms, it cannot be said that he has dyslexia. If such symptoms are present in a child for reasons other than dyslexia, in many cases, the symptoms of dyslexia may subside or go away with age and with proper training techniques and exercises.

Types

There are usually three types of dyslexia (British Dyslexia Association, 2007; The Rose Report, 2009) by nature and character. These include:

. **Verbal Processing**

- Children have difficulty speaking or expressing language properly with a combination of words and sounds.
- The words or sounds seem very similar and confusing to the child. The child also has difficulty understanding new words.
- The child finds it difficult to copy anything from the board.
- The child's handwriting is too tangled or messy in nature.
- The child may have difficulty finding and understanding missing or hidden words.

b. **Motor Processing**

- The child has difficulty in achieving and coordinating gross motor skills (such as running, standing, swapping place in the play, shrugging shoulders, moving legs) and fine motor skills (e.g., moving fingers, holding a pencil or pen, exchanging balls in play). As a result, he finds it difficult to understand and follow plan-based and sequential steps in games or rhymes.

- In particular, the child's ability to use the fine motor is impaired; for example, the child may have speech delays or difficulty in speaking to learn language due to difficulties in the movement and coordination of the trachea and facial muscles with the brain.

c. Phonological Processing

- The procedural aspect of phonological processing is related to the difficulty of general linguistic expression.
- The child has a weakness in identifying single sounds (Phonetic Awareness: the ability to recognize, identify, and think of the singular sounds within words) and the ability to recognize and perceive differences in sound composition, spoken pronunciation, and individual differences. Children have difficulty deciphering and comprehending words, reading spontaneous rhyme words, reciting rhymes, spelling, expanding vocabulary, and providing written forms of thought.
- In this case, the child has difficulty in incorporating letters with sound, relating, and combining words with sounds, pronouncing letters and syllables with words,

and relating sentences with words and paragraphs with sentences. Therefore, they have difficulty pronouncing sounds and letters and spelling words. Some sounds they do not notice or grasp. Do not perceive the rhythmic stages or endings of the rhyme. The child cannot assimilate the sequential phases or ending similarities of a rhyme.

- Sometimes, children have difficulty understanding the first or last sound or letter of a word, so they may miss certain letters. such as the English word cat is called at, and alternative words such as tea is called sea. Weakness in expressing phonological processing may have a strong link with weak short-term memory in children. Any one or two or three of the above types are observed in children with dyslexia.

Causes

Children are born with dyslexia, and it lasts a lifetime (Chievers, 2001).

The following factors (Ibid., 2001; Davis & Braun, 1994; Williams & Lynch, 2010; The Rose Report, 2009; Lucid Research, 2006; Nordqvist, 2016; The National Centre for Learning Disabilities, 2014; Shywiz, 1996; Snowling, 2000; Snowling, 2012) are associated with dyslexia:

- Dyslexia can occur if the mother has labor pains for more than 36 hours at the child's birth and if the child is deprived of oxygen at birth.

- It is also caused by a defect in the nervous system.

- If the child is born prematurely.

- If a child is under weighting at birth.

- The child may also have dyslexia if the parents, siblings, or someone else in the family have dyslexia.

- If the parents are not literate, there may be problems with the expression of reading skills in the child.

- In many cases, if English is taught as a second or third language of a country or as a foreign language, then the child will have difficulty reading English, although this may not be the case when learning the native language.

- Gene DCDC-2, which is thought to be associated with impaired readability. Furthermore, scientists believe that there may be a possibility of having dyslexia with shortening or mutation of chromosomes 1,2,3,6,11,14,15.

- Dyslexia can occur if the child has a short-term memory problem.

When it is possible to pinpoint the exact cause of a child's dyslexia, it is easier to apply proper identification methods and learning techniques.

Diagnosis Methods

The following tests may be used to diagnose dyslexia (Chievers, 2001):

- Aston Index Assessment: for 5-14 years old.
- Cognitive Profiling System: for 4-8 years old.
- Dyslexia Early Screenings Test (DEST): for 4-6 and 6 months old.
- Dyslexia Adult Screenings Test: 16 years and 6 months old.
- Lucid Assessment System for School: for 11-15 years old.
- Phonological Assessment Battery: for 6-14 years old.
- Educational psychologist report: For any age.

Appropriate techniques can be used to improve a child's learning skills by identifying and determining the level of dyslexia through appropriate tests.

Learning Techniques

Different helpful strategies (Chievers, 2001; The Rose Report, 2009; Lucid Research, 2006; Nordqvist, 2016; The National Centre for Learning Disabilities, 2014; Shywiz, 1996; Snowling,

2000; Snowling, 2012; Jaka, 2015) can be applied to the development of learning skills in children with dyslexia, such as:

- Providing vitamins (iron, zinc, and multivitamins).
- Provide extra time and instruction during the lesson and try to teach the lesson individually (10–20 minutes).
- Applying a multi-sensory integration approach through using auditory, visual and kinesthetic learning styles together to continue the learning process.
- The learning process can be continued by combining the use of images with phonological processing through phonographics.
- Applying play activities such as: Distinct types of games such as Ludo, board games, Kin's games, Doll games, guessing games and rhyme-poems, role play to teach the lesson to the child.
- Apply physiotherapy to improve motor movement and coordination skills.
- Provide neurofeedback, neuromodulation, and audio-visual entrainment therapies to train the brain to become more active.
- Alphabet, rhyme, and other reading-related learning can be provided through various applications of computers, mobile devices, tablets, word processors, and Google Play.

- Apply individual education plan-based learning to children.

The level of learning ability of children with dyslexia develops significantly when the right learning techniques are applied over a specific period of time at the right time and age. Children with dyslexia have some basic abilities (Davis & Braun, 1994), such as:

- They can use the brain's basic ability to instinctively be alert and perceive things.
- They are very careful about the surrounding environment.
- They are more interested and inquisitive than average.
- They like to learn more with pictures than with the use of words.
- Instinctively, they are observant and far-sighted.
- They use all the senses to think and observe through multi-sense activities.
- They can provide a real form of thinking.
- They have multiple imaginative tendencies, so creative and innovative propensities are very strong in them.

If children with dyslexia can be supported to identify and enhance to be more basic abilities, both in the family environment and in the educational system, then their social lives can be compelled to be more functional and enjoyable.

References

Armstrong, D., & Humphrey, N. (2008). Reaction to a diagnosis of dyslexia among students entering further education: Development of the resistance accommodation model. *British Journal of Special Education, 36(3), 96-106.*

Avlidou, D. M. (2015). The Educational, Social and Emotional Experiences of Students with Dyslexia: the perspectives of post-secondary education students. *International Journal of Special Education, 30(1).*

Chivers, M. (2001). *Practical Strategies for Living with Dyslexia.* London: Jessica Kingsley Publishers.

Davis, R. D., & Braun, E. (1994). *The Gift of Dyslexia. What dyslexia really is. Part One.* London: A Perigee Book.

Jaka, S. F. (2015). Head Teachers and Teachers as Pioneers in Facilitating Dyslexic Children in Primary Mainstream Schools. *Journal of Education and Educational Development, 2(2), 172-190.*

Lucid Research. (2006). Understanding Dyslexia. Lucid Research, Fact Sheet-19, 1-3. www.lucid-research.com

Macintyre, C. (2002). Play for Children with Special Needs. London: David Fulton Publishers.

National Center for Learning Disabilities. (2014). The power to hope, to learn, and to succeed. The State of Learning's Disabilities. Facts, Trends, and Emerging Issues. 3rd ed. New York, NY: NCLD.

Nordqvist, C. (2016). Dyslexia, Causes, Symptoms and Treatments. https://www.medicalnewstoday.com/search?q=dyslexia

Shastry. (2007), cited in Williams, J.A., & Lynch, S.A. (2010). Dyslexia: What teachers need to know. *Kappa Delta Pi Record. 46(2), 66-70.*

Shaywitz, E. S. (1996). Paradox of Dyslexia. *Scientific American. November: 1996,* 99-105.

Snowling, J. M. (2000). *Dyslexia.* 2nd ed. London: Black Wall.

Snowling, J. M. (2012). Early Identifications and Interventions for dyslexia. A contemporary view. *Journal of Research in Special Needs, 13(1), 7-14.*

The Rose Report. June (2009). *Identifying and Teaching Children and Young People with Dyslexia and Literacy Difficulties.* An independent report from Sir Jim Rose to the

Secretary of State for Children, Schools, and Families
(DSCF). United Kingdom.

Vance, M. & Mitchell, E. (2006). Short Term Memory
Assessment
and Intervention. In J. Snowling Stockhouse, J.
Stockhouse (Eds. *Dyslexia Speech and Languages.* West
Sussex: Whurr Publications Limited.

Waller, E., et al., Al (2000). *Day to Day Dyslexia in Classroom.*
London: Routledge.

Williams, J.A., & Lynch, S.A. (2010). Dyslexia: What teachers
need to know? *Kappa Delta Pi Record. 46(2),* 66-70.

DYSPRAXIA

CHAPTER 3

Dyspraxia: Motor Movement Difficulty

Dyspraxia is a neurological-based specific learning disability (Australian Dyspraxia Association, 2015; Dyspraxia Foundation, USA, 2016), which is inextricably linked with impaired motor coordination or physical movement in a child with the immature brain (Ibid., 2016; Dyspraxia Foundation, UK, 2016; Dyspraxia Checklist, 2016). The term dyspraxia is derived from the Latin word "dys," which means "weak", and "praxis", which means weakness due to coordination (motor movement) (Dorfman, 2007).

During the psych-physical development, when a child has difficulty developing a specific well-planned and sequential task and has difficulty in speaking or performing daily tasks with a combination of gross and fine motor skills, it is called dyspraxia (Dyspraxia Foundation, UK, 2016; Patino, 2017). Dyspraxia is also called motor coordination disability.

A child with dyspraxia has a weakened immune system, and the nervous system is damaged. Therefore, children with dyspraxia may be slow or fail to achieve developmental stages, such as lifting their necks, sitting, crawling, walking, and speaking. Currently, two out of every one hundred children have dyspraxia, and dyspraxia is relatively more common in boys (Dyspraxia Checklist, 2016). It is present in the baby from birth, is associated with the primary motor cortex of the brain, and lasts a lifetime (Patino, 2007; Australian Dyspraxia Association, 2016). However, if a stroke or any other brain injury occurs in life, it happens in adults. Usually, a child with dyspraxia has poor memory, forgets things, and often loses things. Detection of dyspraxia before 5 years of age may be mistaken for autism or dyslexia (The National Health Service, 2016). However, dyspraxia may be exacerbated by inattention or hyperactivity, autism, dyslexia, and cerebral palsy (Dyspraxia Foundation, USA, 2016). Dyspraxia is often considered a form of dyslexia (Addz, 2003; Dyspraxia Association, UK, 2016; Patino, 2017). Bill Gates, Harry Potter actor Daniel Radcliffe, scientist Isaac Newton, and painter Pablo Picasso are some of the prominent figures in dyspraxia (Simpson, 2016).

Characteristics and Types

There are three main types of dyspraxia (Australian Dyspraxia Association, 2015; Health Direct, 2016), depending on the characteristics demonstrated by children, such as:

a. Motor Dyspraxia

Children with motor dyspraxia may not be able to or may have difficulty performing simple organizational and periodic tasks through motor movement according to age. These include:

- **Performing organizational tasks through gross motor movements:** Having difficulty sitting, walking, standing, running, maintaining body balance with head and shoulders or legs; feeling difficult or inconvenient to climb stairs; having trouble writing or drawing by hand.

- **Performing sequential tasks through gross motor movements:** Having trouble sitting in a chair during meals; Problems wearing clothes or not being able to stand on one leg while wearing clothes; Having trouble catching and throwing the ball; There is difficulty in brushing teeth; Not understanding to make bed or go to sleep; Not being able to use the toilet on her own; Unable to understand geometric drawings or concepts of distance or making building blocks.

- **Performing tasks through fine motor movements:** Having difficulty attaching shoelaces with fingers; having difficulty eating with a fork or spoon; having trouble holding a pen or pencil; have trouble in writing; having difficulty wearing shirt buttons or pants zipper; cannot comb hair and can't wave hands.

b. Oral Dyspraxia

Children with oral dyspraxia may not be able to properly coordinate their tongue, lip movements, and facial muscles. As a result, the child cannot chew, suck, lick, or bite according to age. The baby cannot blow out the candle with Fu or eat ice cream with tongue.

c. Verbal Dyspraxia

Verbal dyspraxia is called childhood apraxia of speech. In this case, the child is unable to utter words through the movement of muscles, so that he cannot transmit information to communicate with the brain and other parts of the body, can't perform sequential or periodic thinking and augmentation, and can't use physical techniques to speak or speak late, or even if he speaks, words disappear or words may seem incomprehensible. Usually, children cannot utter a word until they are three years old. The child cannot imitate others or himself in the mirror as a prerequisite for speaking according to age.

Symptoms

The following symptoms appear in children with dyspraxia at different ages (NHS, 2016, Dyspraxia Foundation, USA):

a. **0-3 Years of age**

- Children with dyspraxia have some annoying behaviors from birth (sudden crying at night, trouble sleeping, tingling, or biting others when they are a little older, and biting their own hands when excited, hitting the floor with their heads) and have trouble eating (indigestion, difficulty in breastfeeding, hiccups, loss of appetite, frequent vomiting after eating, difficulty swallowing and chewing, and sucking food).

- They achieve the developmental stages of the learning process very slowly. For example, they cannot sit on their own until they are eight or nine months old, many cannot crawl or too late, for a long time before learning to walk they walk on the floor by the bottom of the body or on the chest, and after learning to walk they rub their feet on the soles of the feet and speak late.

b. **Pre-school or 3-5 Years of age**

If a child's dyspraxia is not diagnosed before the age of three, then the child's psycho-physical problems become apparent as he enters school life, and his self-confidence is shattered, leaving him frustrated and unable to adapt to the school environment.

Children with dyspraxia between the ages of three and five develop the following symptoms:

- The baby has trouble sitting still, and he may move his arms and legs unnecessarily.
- Express excitement with loud, sharp, hoarse voices.
- Too early to become impatient, angry, frustrated, and depressed.
- Often stumbles or falls on another person or thing.
- When running, the child flutters his or her hands like a bird's wings and grabs or pinches another with its hand.
- These children cannot ride bicycles or toys like that.
- Such children are not self-aware and are unaware of impending danger, such as difficulty walking on the road or in high places.
- Children find it difficult to decipher in class.
- When children try to eat with their fingers or hands, food and drinks will fall.
- Difficulty in playing according to age, such as constructive games (puzzle games, building blocks), imaginative games (playing with hands like an airplane) and creative games.

- The child has problems interacting and playing with peers and is often isolated from others, but is more interested in interacting with adults and prefers the company of adults.

- The dominance of the left hand and the right hand is unclear.

- The child has speech delays or trouble speaking.

- The child develops hypersensitivity to the senses, such as too much noise or unexpected sound or darkness or fear of a crowd of people or a new guest.

- Not being able to wear clothes, brushing, using the toilet, and combing the hair.

- The child has difficulty following verbal instructions, has difficulty responding, and has difficulty understanding anything.

- The child lacks concentration and cannot finish classwork.

- The child's memory is impaired, forgets the names of things, and often loses valuable things.

c. 5-7 years of age

- Children cannot adapt to school routines or rules.

- The child's listening and speaking skills are poor.

- The child has trouble remembering two or more verbal

instructions.

- The child deciphers very slowly.
- The child moves too much body and muscle.
- The child shakes or bites hands when excited.
- The child becomes mentally and emotionally disturbed very quickly.
- Children cannot eat with knives and cutlery or with their hands.
- Children cannot make friendships with their peers.
- The child may have trouble sleeping, wake up suddenly, start crying, or wake up with nightmares.
- The child has problems with migraines, headaches, abdominal pain, and feeling sick all of a sudden.

d. 8-9 Years of age

Handwriting is vague and can have the above problems as well.

Causes

The reasons for dyspraxia (NHS, 2016) are as follows:

- When a child is born prematurely (gestational age is less than 37 weeks), the immature brain cannot maintain contact with the nervous system through its nerve cells or fails to communicate with the body's motors or muscle system. This causes problems in the development of the child's learning process.

- If the child weighs less at birth.
- If the child lacks adequate oxygen at birth.
- If the child has any infectious disease at birth.
- If the mother takes excessive amounts of drugs during pregnancy.
- In adults, a person suffering from a stroke or a brain injury due to an accident can develop dyspraxia.

Diagnosis Methods

Dyspraxia can be largely identified by its features and symptoms. Moreover, it is possible to become aware of the immature brain through Computed Tomography Scan (CT scan), Magnetic Resonance Imaging (MRI), and Positron Emission Tomography.

Learning Techniques

Dyspraxia cannot be completely eradicated (NHS, 2016; Dyspraxia Foundation, USA, 2016; Nordqvist, 2016; Boon, 2001; Macintyre, 2002; Dorfman, 2007). However, the following strategies can be applied to increase maturation of the brain:

- taking drugs that increase the maturation of the brain, taking iron and zinc, calcium-rich vitamins.

- Provide psychotherapy/ Cognitive Behavioral Therapy/ counseling with the help of educational and child psychologists.
- Provide speech therapy.
- Provide physiotherapy and occupational therapy.
- Provide social integration therapy.
- Apply oral stimulator.
- Increase brain performance through neurofeedback and neuromodulation therapies.
- Arranging play activities. Apply different types of games, such as Ludo, board games, kins games, puppet games, guessing games and rhymes, poetry, and role play to teach the child class lessons.

Applying proper healthcare and learning strategies as needed can positively improve the learning process of a child with dyspraxia.

References

Addy, L.M. (2003). *How to Understand and Support Children with Dyspraxia.* Cambridge: LDA.

Australian Dyspraxia Association Inc. (2016). *Dyspraxia, Difficulties Coalition.* www.dyspraxia.com.au/

Boon, M. (2001). *Helping Children with Dyspraxia.* London: Jessica Kingsley Publisher's Ltd.

Dorfman, K. (2007). The Best Dyspraxia Program Ever. Developmental Delay Resources. The One Resource Network Integrating Conventional and Holistic Approach. *Nutrition, New Developments. 12:6.*

Dyspraxia Checklist. Assessment and Diagnosis. (2016).

Dyspraxia Foundation UK. 2016. *Dyspraxia-Children.* Hitching, United Kingdom.

https://www.dyspraxiafoundation.org.uk

Dyspraxia Foundation USA. (2015). Understand, Support and Accept. "1 in 10" odds are you know someone with Dyspraxia.

www.dyspraxiausa.org

Health Service Executive—Ireland. (n.d.). *Developmental Coordination Disorders.*

https://www.hse.ie/eng/health/as/D/Developmental_C
o_ordination_Disorders/causes_of_dyspraxia

Macintyre, C. (2002). *Play for Children with Special Needs.*

London: David Fulton Publishers.

Nordqvist, C. (2016). *Dyspraxia: Causes, Symptoms and*

Treatment. Pediatric Children's Health.

https://www.medicalnewstoday.com/articles/151951.p
hp%22.php

Patino, E. (2017). *Understanding Dyspraxia. Parent Toolkit.*

www.understood.org/en/learning-attention-
issues/child-learning-disabilities

Simpson, A. (2016). *A list of Famous People with Dyspraxia.*

https://www.antonysimpson.com/a_list_of_famous_pe
ople_with_dyspraxia_dyslexia

The National Health Service (NHS), United Kingdom. (2016).

Developmental Coordination Disorders in (dyspraxia) Children.

www.NHS.UK/conditions/dyspraxia

DYSGRAPHIA

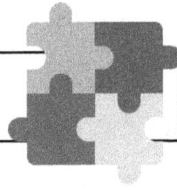

CHAPTER 4

Dysgraphia: Writing Difficulty

Dysgraphia is a neurodevelopmental learning disability that impairs a child's ability or skill to write (King & Easther, 2015). The physical structural features of writing are impaired in children with dysgraphia. For example, a strong fist to hold a pencil is inconsistent or weak, handwriting is very vague, the child has difficulty in offering a written form of thinking, and the child misspells words (Richards, 1999). In addition, the child feels problems in performing fine motor skills for writing properly. As a result, handwriting is inconsistent or obscure (King & Easther, 2015; The International Dyslexia Association, 2000).

Many children find writing difficult because of dysgraphia and avoid writing out of frustration (Ibid., 2015). Dysgraphia is often misinterpreted with other learning disabilities such as dyslexia, dysphagia, speech delay, inattention, and severe restlessness.

Many children with dyslexia may have dysgraphia, and children may have dysgraphia even if they do not have dyslexia (The International Dyslexia Association, 2000). Famous writer Agatha Christie, scientist Alva Edison and Albert Einstein, and others had dysgraphia difficulties in their lives (Famous People with Dysgraphia, 2016).

Characteristics and Symptoms

The following features and symptoms (Richards, 1999; King & Easther, 2015; The International Dyslexia Association, 2000; Crouch & Jakubecy, 2007; Martins et al., 2013) are commonly observed in children with dysgraphia:

- The child's handwriting is blurred, meaning that the child is unable to write clearly and has difficulty writing in a well-organized or coherent way.
- The child finds it very difficult to write and feels pain in the arm while writing.
- At the time of writing, the child's fingers get stuck in the pen or pencil, and the child feels numb in writing, thus disrupting the automatic speed of writing.
- When writing, the position of the child's wrist, body, and the position of the paper stay unequal; as a result, the child's physical expression seems inconsistent.
- Having difficulty writing letters means that the child has difficulty constructing the structure and putting on the shape of the letters correctly.
- Forming letters irregularly, inconsistently, and diagonally.

- There is a problem with the proper spacing between letters and words.
- Making an unnecessary combination of lowercase and uppercase letters in the same word.
- Combining printed and cursive handwriting in the same word or sentence.
- Unnecessary tendency to repeatedly delete letters or words with a pencil. Words or letters are written that are too cursive and incomplete, and words or letters deviate or disappear.
- Children tend to see the text very closely.
- Child's writing speed is very slow in nature.
- The child has a tendency to misspell or use unknown or erroneous words in sentences.
- The child writes the letter in reverse or after the previous letter.
- The child has problems with the proper use of lines and margins.
- There are problems with turning the page properly.
- There are grammatical errors in syntax.
- The baby's copying speed is very slow or cannot be copied at all.
- Children may find it difficult to pay attention when writing, especially when they become inattentive or

forget about details.

- The child has difficulty understanding the sequential and planned verbal instructions and follows them very slowly.

- Extra verbal guidance is always needed for the baby.

- The child takes extra time for classroom lessons, so the child's spontaneous participation in the lesson activities is very low, and the homework remains incomplete or cannot be completed.

Causes

- Dysgraphia can occur when the part of the brain that carries organizational activity is damaged or inconsistent. The brain has two main types of information-exchange processes. For example, children find it difficult to write when there is an obstacle in passing the process of sound or pronunciation to reach the written stage and at the same time find it difficult to deliver the written form of mental thinking.

- Distracting attention, memory retention, and difficulty transcribing instructive elements of pictorial information can lead to dysgraphia.

- Handwriting may be blurred if the child has problems with fine motor movement or coordination. Many times, the child feels physical vibrations and blooming, which impairs his or her ability to write.

- The coexistence of any other difficulty may cause dysgraphia in children. For example, if a child has a problem with fine motor movement, he or she may have difficulty retrieving or revisualizing a letter or a set of letters, resulting in difficulty remembering the letter structure or type (Rostami et al., 2014; The International Dyslexia Association, 2000).

Types

There are usually three types of dysgraphia:

a. **Dyslexic Dysgraphia**

The handwriting of a child with dyslexia is very vague. In this case, the child cannot write anything spontaneously. Especially if the text is a very complex type, he will not be able to grasp its meaning. Moreover, the child has very few spelling skills, but they are very good at drawing. The child's ability to copy a written text is relatively good, and the speed of pencil holding and writing through fine motor coordination or with the finger is normal.

b. **Motor Dysgraphia**

The handwriting of a child with motor dystrophy is

blurred, and the child has less ability to write and copy texts spontaneously. Although spelling skills are good, drawing skills are very weak. The capability and speed of holding the pencil with the finger is very weak, so the pencil is mistakenly held and the writing becomes crooked.

c. **Spatial Dysgraphia**

In this case the child's handwriting is very vague and the child has difficulty in writing. Although children are good at spelling and holding a pencil with their fingers, they have difficulty drawing. The child has difficulty seeing the position of the letters and does not understand the concepts of volume, density, and distance (The International Dyslexia Association, 2000).

In addition to the above three types, there are two types of dysgraphia based on the ability to write:

a. **Expressive Writing**

In this case, some mental stages (such as organizational ability, memory, attention, motor skills and language skills) must be passed to acquire the writing stage and the child finds it difficult to go beyond these stages to the writing stage, resulting in blurred handwriting.

b. Automatic Writing

If there is a problem beyond the mental stages, the child will not be competent to write automatically. Children do not automatically understand how to hold a pencil, where to hold it, and how to write letters, as well as not being able to remember how to articulate written expression or write the text. Children with dysgraphia have distorted ability to attain and exemplify expressive and automatic writing.

Diagnosis Methods

There is not any specific medical protocol for diagnosing dysgraphia and it is not even possible to diagnose it by Brain Imaging Technology. However, psychiatrists and special education psychologists can diagnose dysgraphia through a variety of assessment tests (Knobelauch, 2008). These include:

- The WISE-IV Processing Speed Index Score.
- Visual-Motor Integration Developmental Test.
- Bender-Gestalt Test.
- Jordan Left-Right Reversal Test.
- The Halstead Reitan Neuro-physiological Battery Trails Test.

The above tests can be used to observe the child's following abilities (The International Dyslexia Association, 2000):

- Ability to write words or sentences correctly on their own.
- Ability to form paragraphs.
- Ability to copy age-appropriate text.
- Ability to move hands according to the child's pencil holding type, position, hand vibration, and capability of vision.
- Ability to move the fingers or bend the shoulders with the speed of subtle fine motor movement, etc.

Learning Techniques

The following learning techniques (Richards, 1999; The International Dyslexia association, 2000; Crouch & Jakubecy, 2007; Martins, et al., 2013; King & Easther, 2015) can be used to support children with dysgraphia:

- Physiotherapy can enhance fine motor performance.
- Practice handwriting with different triangular pencils or pens through occupational therapy.
- Perform regular finger and hand exercises to improve fine motor coordination skills.
- Use typewriters, mobiles, computers, and touchscreen tablets for writing.
- Provide extra time through writing with a word processor

by following a precise step.

- Enhancing the function of the occipital lobe of the brain through neurofeedback and neuro modulation therapy.
- Practice cursive handwriting very often so that the child can understand the difference between b and d, I and l, p and q, etc.
- Constantly rub both hands together for a specific period of time and rub the hands with regular tennis balls.
- Rub both hands together on the carpet or floor.
- Jump with a small rope.
- Wreath with flowers or small round beads.
- Rubbing hands with soil or mud.
- Rub the top-bottom of the pencil with fingers.

Applying appropriate learning techniques at the right time can encourage a child with dysgraphia to cultivate writing skills as well as reduce writing problems.

References

Crouch, L.A & Jackubecy, J.J. January (2007). Dysgraphia. How it affects it. Case studies. *Teachers Exceptional Children Plus, 0-3(3).* Famous People with Dysgraphia (n.d.). https://healthresearchfunding.org/famous-people-dependent-personality-disorder/

M. King'endo & Easther N, N. (2015). Teaching Learners with Dysgraphia in Primary School in EMBU County, Kenya: Implications for Educational Interventions. Area of Emotional and Behavior Disorders. *International Journal of Educational Research,* 3, 115-123.

Knowbelauch, L. (2008). *How to assist a student with Dysgraphia in the classroom.* www.superduperinc.com/

Martins, M. R. I., et al., (2013). Screening for motor dysgraphia in public schools. Jornal de pediatria (Ria-J), *Sociadade Brasileira de Pediatria,* 89(1), 70-74. www.jped.com.br

Richards, R. (1999). *The Source for Dyslexia and Dysgraphia.* East Moline, IL: Lingui Systems.

Rostami et al., (February 2014). Dysgraphia: The causes and solutions. Exploring Intellectual Capital. *International*

Journal of Academic Research in Business and Social Sciences. 4(2).

The International Dyslexia Association. (2000). *Dysgraphia promotes literacy through research, education, and advocacy.* Fact sheet, 82-01/00. https://dyslexiaida.org

DYSCALCULIA

CHAPTER 5
Dyscalculia: Difficulty in Counting

The term dyscalculia is derived from the Latin word "dys" meaning "difficulty" and the Greek word "calculus", meaning "calculation". (Adler, 2008). The combined meaning of which is "difficulty in counting". In 1940, at first, a German named Gertsman used the term dyscalculia to describe specific or special learning difficulties in mathematics. However, a scientist from the United States first produced the idea of developmental dyscalculia in 1960. When a child's learning process is disrupted due to difficulty in calculating, it can be called dyscalculia (Ibid., 2008). However, the child has difficulty in expressing number or counting so dyscalculia is called number blindness (Butterworth, 2003).

Characteristics

The following features (Butterworth, 1999; Butterworth, 2003; DfES, 2001; Shalev, 2004; Poustie et al., 2001; Kaufman, et al., 2012) are commonly observed in children with dyscalculia:

- Experiencing specific problems in doing math or calculations despite having normal intelligence Especially in arithmetic, the weakness of the child is more noticeable.

- Having difficulty in performing the basic four natures of mathematics (addition, subtraction, multiplication, and division) or taking extra time.

- Counting speed is very slow so children with dyscalculia should be taught according to their cognitive development stage.

- 20-30% of children with dyscalculia have difficulty in reading and writing along with counting problems. Therefore, some people think it is a typical type of dyslexia.

- Children cannot memorize theoretical calculations or numbers. There are many difficulties in performing simple and concise instructional tasks while taking lessons. Despite having normal intelligence, children show unequal results in intellectual tests. However, the cause of these difficulties is not common emotional or psychological but is related to perception or thought process.

- It is difficult for a child to understand and tell real time by looking at a clock. However, children can understand the digital clock comparatively better than the analog clock.

- The child has difficulty in visual perception, regular working memory and in expressing language skills to understand time or calculation.

- Due to poor memory, the child not only forgets what to do, but also forgets about social meetings with others.

- The child has difficulty in calculating or understanding the price of any item and in exchanging money, for example, The child has difficulty in calculating or understanding the price of any item and in exchanging money, for example, the child can't understand the difference between the price of one liter of milk is 10 taka or 50 taka.

- If the child is instructed to do three things, he or she can only remember the last instruction.

- They have problems in performing sequential tasks according to the plan.

- They do not understand the concept of temperature or speed.

Symptoms

(Butterworth, 1999; Adler, 2008; Landerl et al., 2004)

a. Difficulty in Reading

- Children with dyscalculia get confused when reading the numbers that look the same - for example, - 6 as 3, 1 as

7, 6 as 9.

- The child does not understand the space between the two numbers, such as 917, which is considered to be nine hundred seventeen.

- The children make mistakes in using the number sign or symbols (+, -, x, %).

- Children find it difficult to count more than one unit and cannot count numbers by adding zeros. For example, 1004, 7069.

- children read from right to left without counting from left to right. Such as, assume 12 as 21.

- The child cannot provide mathematical explanations for maps, diagrams, or tables.

b. Difficulty in Writing

- Children reverse the number in written form. such as, if it is said, "12" children will write it as 21.

- children cannot copy mathematical symbols and geometric figures and cannot remember the symbols.

- Children find it difficult to write more than one single completed number, such as 1007 to 107 write, 4535 to write separately as 4000, 500, 35.

c. Difficulty in understanding mathematical concepts and symbols.

- Children find it difficult to understand, memorize and use mathematical symbols properly.

- The child has difficulty in understanding the concept of weight, direction, time, and place.

- The child cannot comprehend the concept of how to count. For example, some children, from a few of them to as well as many, cannot understand the difference between the ideas. Moreover, the child has difficulty in understanding the unit of measurement, from centimeter to meter, from meter to kilometer.

- Children do not understand psychological calculations; they use fingers in basic calculations.

- Children cannot understand the sequential calculation, as such: they can't understand why it is called first, second, third, and more. They cannot understand the sequential place of any number, such as: they can't understand how 17 comes after 16.

- Children cannot understand the backward and forward position of serial numbers, such as: they can't understand how the number 25 is less than 5, the number 30 and more than 5, the number 20 and so on.

- The child has difficulty in understanding the practical application of mathematics. For example, if Rahima lives one kilometer away from the market and Karim lives three times away from Rahima, then the child cannot understand how far Karim is from the market.

d. **Difficulty in understanding complex thinking and flexibility.**

- The child cannot comprehend problem-solving math or arithmetic exercises. The child cannot understand the various planning and sequential phases of mathematical practice or solution.
- Children cannot do logical analysis and draft calculations or practice to solve a mathematical problem.

Other Mathematical Difficulties and Dyscalculia

Dyscalculia differs significantly from many other types of mathematical problems (Adler, 2008).

Such as:

a. **Acalculia**

Children with acalculia cannot count at all. They cannot even calculate the counting up to 1-10 or the innate phase of 1 + 1 = 2, 2 + 2 = 4.

b. **General difficulties in mathematics**

Usually, children with delayed development have such problems. The development of mathematical concepts in them is very slow in nature but they are much higher in calculation and cognitive ability than in children with dyscalculia. Usually, if they are given extra time during the lesson, their problem will be reduced to a greater extent.

c. **Pseudo Dyscalculia**

Different emotional barriers, such as past failures, unwanted pre-experience, and lack of motivation in the classroom are the source of such problems. These children usually have problems with counting due to emotional barriers. They are driven by emotion and predict that they will not be able to succeed in mathematics, as a result of which their self-confidence will decrease and they will not be able to become proficient in mathematics. Their emotional barriers can be overcome through periodic private secret meetings or professional interviews with educational psychologists, specialized education teachers or professionals, and social workers.

Causes

If the back (parietal lobe) of the baby's brain is damaged, the baby may have dyscalculia (Butterworth, 1999). The parietal lobe leads to the development of mathematical and linguistic skills. The parietal lobe of the child may be damaged due to hereditary, environmental factors, or both (Ibid., 1999).

a. **Genetic causes**

The presence of certain genes before or during pregnancy can be responsible for the dyscalculia of the baby, such as Fragile X syndrome, Williams Baron syndrome, and Val cardio facial syndrome.

b. **Environmental causes**

The child may have dyscalculia if the mother is addicted to drugs during pregnancy, such as: drinking, smoking or taking drugs; if the baby is born prematurely; speech delay; epilepsy, if there is a problem with metabolism.

c. **Both**

The child may develop dyscalculia if various parts of the child's brain are affected at the same time due to both hereditary and environmental factors.

In addition to other learning disabilities, the child may have dyscalculia, such as dyslexia, dyspraxia, inattention and restlessness, specific language barriers, and other learning difficulties.

Types

There are usually three types of dyscalculia (Dyscalculia in Ireland, n.d.):

a. **Quantitative Dyscalculia**

Children with such dyscalculia have difficulty calculating and keeping quantitative calculations.

b. **Qualitative Dyscalculia**

In this case, the child finds it difficult to explain any mathematical practice, solve problems and acquire mathematical skills by following the verbal instructions. For example, they cannot provide mathematical explanations according to the symbols of addition, subtraction, multiplication, division, and square root concept.

c. **Intermediate Dyscalculia**

Children with intermediate dyscalculia have difficulty expressing mathematical symbols and quantitative calculations, that is, both numerical and qualitative concepts.

Diagnosis

The best time to diagnose dyscalculia is usually between 10 and 12 years of age (Adler, 2008). By looking at the features and symptoms, it can be detected that the child has dyscalculia. In this case the dyscalculia screening test (Butterworth, 2003) can be followed. Along with it, brain imaging technology such as computer tomography or MRI to find out if the peritoneal lobe of the baby's brain is damaged, it is possible to know if there is dyscalculia.

Learning Techniques

Dyscalculia can be largely cured by applying appropriate learning strategies over several consecutive years. The following strategies (Butterworth, 1999; DfES, 2001; Cohen et al., 2010) can be used to develop the learning skills of a child with dyscalculia:

- An individualized approach or Personalized Learning Approach can be applied by providing extra time through a teaching assistant which increases the child's math practice skills.

- Neurofeedback and Neuro Modulation therapies can be used to increase a baby's brain function.

- Dyscalculia cannot be eliminated by taking any specific medication. However, vitamins and brain-enhancing drugs help reduce the child's fears and anxieties about math.

- Psychotherapy can be provided.

Applying appropriate techniques at the right time by following specific mathematical exercises over a period of time can greatly reduce the level of dyscalculia in a child.

References

Adler, B. (2001). Revised, 2008. *What is dyscalculia?* Cognitive Centre in Sweden.

Butterworth, B. (1999). *The Mathematical Brain.* London: McMillan.

Butterworth, B. (2003). *Dyscalculia Screener. Highlighting Pupils with Specific Learning Difficulties in Math's. Age 6-14 years.* London: Fenelon Publishing Company Limited.

Cohen, K. et al., (2010). Modulating neural activity produces specific and long-lasting changes in numerical competence. *Current Biology, 20*(22), 2016-2020.

DfES. (2001). *Guidance to Support with Dyslexia and Dyscalculia.* London: Department of Education & Skills.

Dyslexia in Ireland. (n.d.). www.edubloxtutor.com

Kaufmann, L., et al., (2012). *Deutsches Ärzteblatt International.* Berlin, Germany. www.ncbi.nlm.nih.gov

Landerl, K., Bevan. A., & Butterworth, B. (2004). Developmental dyscalculia and basic numerical capacities: A study of 8-9 years old students. *Cognition, 93,* 99-125.

Poustie, J. et al., (2001). *Mathematics Solution: An Introduction to Dyscalculia*. Next Generation.

Shalev, R. (2004). Developmental Dyscalculia. *Journal of Child Neurology, 49*(11), 868-87.

DEVELOPMENTAL DELAY

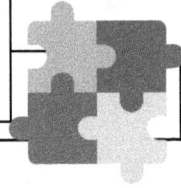

CHAPTER 6

Developmental Delay: Difficulty in Achieving Developmental Stages

Developmental delay can be termed as delays in achieving specific psycho-physical developmental stages in children under five years of age, such as motor skills, speech and language skills, personal and social skills, and daily performance skills (Shevell et al., 2003; O'Byrne, 2015).

Developmental delays are observed in many cases, varying from neurological disorders to motor coordination difficulties and specific learning disabilities.

Characteristics and Symptoms

Every child has a certain speed or stage in achieving psychophysical development. Significant delays in the development of some of the major abilities or skill stages in acquiring the learning process can be considered developmental delays in children compared to their peers (Sachdeva, 2010; Walters, 2010; Parna & Laugan, 2013; AAN & CNS, n.d.).

Such as:

a. **Gross Motor and Fine Motor Skill Development**

The child may have difficulty or delay in sitting, walking, standing, running, maintaining balance, and shifting position through the movement of the gross motor. In the case of fine motor skills movement children find it difficult to eat by hands and fingers movements, holding pencil, painting, drawing, dressing, writing, and following instructions to play stage-based games.

b. **Cognitive Development**

The child experiences difficulty or delay in achieving cognitive skills, such as the ability to understand or learn the learning process, self-control, individuality, problem-solving and reasoning decision-making ability, memory skills development.

c. **Daily Activities Performing**

Usually, if there is a problem with motor coordination or the development of the cognitive senses, the child may not be able to perform or delay the daily activities, such as dressing, using the toilet, eating on his own, wearing shoes and other regular activities.

d. Social and Emotional Development

The child may show delay in acquiring the ability to maintain social communication and interaction with family members, teachers, peers, the ability to maintain relationships with others, to respond to the feelings of others and to cooperate with others.

e. Speech and Language Development

Delay or difficulty in speaking or speech development, difficulty in expressing meaningful speech through communication and language gestures, delays in listening, understanding, and responding to others.

When a child shows delays in the acquisition of any one or two of the above five developmental skills, it is called a specific developmental delay. And if there is a delay in the development of more than two or five skills, then it is called global developmental delay (Shavell et al., 2003).

Causes

(AAN & CNS, n.d.; Sachdeva, 2010; Walters, 2010; O'Byrne et al., 2015; Queensland Government, n.d.):

- About 20% of developmental delays, except for neurological and hereditary factors, can lead to delayed development as a result of complications at birth.

- If the baby being born prematurely, weighs less than 2 kg at birth, has severe Jaundice, Down Syndrome, Fragile X Syndrome, Angelman Syndrome, Rett's, Maternal Problems, Phenyl Kutu Neuria, Muscle Malnutrition Problems, and other congenital problems, the baby may be delayed.

- The child with developmental delay may have a variety of environmental causes linked to the mother's health, such as the mother being constantly depressed during pregnancy, smoking, and taking drugs.

- If the child suffers from extreme poverty, neglect, and physical and mental abuse during the postnatal period, he / she may delay the acquisition of learning skills.

- About 1% of children with developmental delays have metabolic problems, such as urea-related disorders, neonatal phenylketonuria, anemia, and dehydration.

- Hypothyroidism before or during birth can lead to delayed development of the baby.

- Brain injury or immature brain before and after birth can lead to delayed development of the baby, such as cerebral palsy.

- Specific learning disabilities and neurological impairments may be responsible for the child's delayed development, as such - dyslexia, dyspraxia, autism, attention deficit hyperactivity disorder, and others.

- If the mother and baby have any infectious disease during pregnancy, such as rubella, chicken pox, HIV, measles in the pregnant mother, or measles in the newborn, the baby may have a delayed development.

- If the mother is exposed to any toxic substance during pregnancy, such as lead or any harmful drug, the child may develop delayed development.

- Seizures, epilepsy, or sensory problems are one of the causes of delayed development.

Diagnosis Methods

- Delayed development can often be identified by examining family history or periodic three lineage data.

- Delayed development can be detected by examining the brains of children 1 to 5 years of age using Neuro-imaging methods, as such computed tomography, Magnetic Resonance Imaging.

- The Electroencephalogram (EEG) device can detect the presence of seizures.

- "Full Blood Count Test" can be done for anemia and iron deficiency.

- Metabolic screening tests can detect problems with serum amino acids, urine organic acids, serum glucose bicarbonate acid, and creatine kinase.

- The Hearing & Vision Test can diagnose vision and hearing problems (AAN & CNS, n.d.; Sachdeva, 2010; Walters, 2010; O'Byrne et al., 2015).

Appropriate learning techniques can be applied to enhance a child's learning ability if the nature of the developmental delay is properly diagnosed through precise identification methods.

Learning Techniques

(AAN & CNS, n.d.; Parna & Laugan, 2013)

- Physiotherapy.
- Play activities, for example, rhyme, sequential game or game with rules, drawing, coloring, and role play.
- Using neurofeedback and neuromodulation therapy to stimulate the inactive cells of the brain.
- Provide speech and language therapy.
- Provide occupational therapy.
- Provide Social Integration Therapy.

Applying appropriate learning strategies, as soon as possible, leads to significant improvement in the learning ability of a child with a developmental delay.

References

Ministry of Communities, Child Safety and Disability Services. Queensland Government. (n.d.). *My Child Has Developmental Delay: information to Queensland families of young children. A Parent Connect Resource.* Queensland, Australia.

O' Byrne, J. J., et al., (2015). Unexplained developmental delay/ learning disability: guidelines for best practice protocol for first line assessment and genetic / metabolic / radiological investigations. *Journal of Medical Science,* 1-8. Spinger, Ireland.

Parna, R., & Laughan, AR, (2013). Early developmental delays. *Journal of Psychological Abnormalities in Children,* 1(2), 1-5.

Sachdeva, S. et al., (2010). Global Developmental Delay and its Determinants among Urban Infant and Toddlers: A Cross Sectional Study. *Indian Journal of Pediatric, 779,* 975-970.

Shevell. M, et al., February (2003). Practice parameters:

evaluation of the child with Global Developmental

Delay. Report of the Quality Standard Subcommittee of

the American Academy of Neurology Society. American

Academy of Neurology. Special Article. *Neurology,*

60(2), 367-380.

The American Academy of Neurology and Child Neurology

Society Guidelines Summary for Clinicians (n.d.).

Evaluation of the Child with Global Developmental

Delay. www.aan.com

The National Early Childhood Technical Assistant Centre

(NECTAC). July 2011. Early Intervention for Infants and

Toddlers with Disabilities and Their Families.

www.nectac.org

Walters. A. (2010). Developmental delay causes and

investigations. Pediatric Neurology, 10(2), 32-34.

CEREBRAL PALSY

CHAPTER 7

Cerebral Palsy: Physical Disability Due to the Immature Brain

Cerebral means "brain" and "palsy", meaning "weakness" or "complete disability". (Bajraszewski et al., 2008). It is a neurological disorder. Due to immature brain or damaged brain triggers Developmental difficulties and dysfunction in the nervous system or transmitted diseases may occur which cause abnormality in usual movement and motor movement that limit their daily activities. This is called cerebral palsy (Disability Rights and Protection Act, 2013; CP Now, 2015; The Center for Children with Special Needs, 2011). It is a permanent disability; however, over time psycho-physical improvement happens in the children, and they may be able to lead a normal life (The Center for Children with Special Needs, 2011).

Cerebral palsy occurs when a child develops abnormal movements and postures due to developmental complications of immature brain and injury or disease of the nervous system that limits his or her daily activities.

Causes

The reason for the birth of cerebral palsy in many children is still unknown. Nevertheless, the researchers agreed that pre-natal, peri-natal, and post-natal conditions are responsible for cerebral palsy in children (CP Now, 2015; The Centre for Children with Special Needs, 2011; Bajraszewski et al., 2008).

a. **Pre-Natal**

In 79-80% of cases, prenatal factors play a vital role in the development of cerebral palsy in children. Due to defective structures of the brain, a pregnant mother's rubella or infectious diseases, bacterial and viral diseases, or if there is any metabolism problem in the mother that may trigger cerebral palsy in the baby.

b. **Peri-Natal**

In 10-15% of cases, perinatal causes are responsible for developing cerebral palsy in children.

Cerebral palsy is more likely to occur if the mother has a very severe labor pain, a mother has seizures or convulsions during childbirth, antepartum hemorrhage, premature birth, low birth weight of 2-5 kg or less than 2500 grams and severe jaundice in a newborn child, or lack of oxygen and circulatory problems at birth.

c. **Post Neonatal**

In 10% of cases of cerebral palsy, the postnatal cause acts as a Catalyst Cerebral Palsy can occur within 28 days of birth if the baby is infected with a contagious disease such as measles or rubella, a stroke, a car accident or drowning, or any other injury to the brain (Disability Rights and Protection Act, 2013; The Centre for Children with Special Needs, 2011).

Symptoms and Characteristics

Usually, the following features and symptoms (Disability Rights and Protection Act, 2013; CP Now, 2015; The Centre for Children with Special Needs, 2011; Bajraszewski, et al., 2008) are more common in children with cerebral palsy:

- The baby's muscles are very stiff or flexible,
- They may feel uncomfortable in movement of hands or feet,
- the baby's normal movement is unbalanced,
- twins or multiple birth, A premature birth [not all premature babies have cerebral palsy, but most cerebral palsy babies born prematurely],
- if the baby weighs less than 2500 grams at birth, there is visual and hearing impairment,
- there are problems with the development of intelligence

and learning skills,

- they may experience convulsions or seizures, Children feel pain in the body or muscles,
- the baby has difficulty in expressing social communication skills,
- the children may have a weakness in expressing behavioral or emotional traits,
- the child may have speech delay or not able to speak or having difficulty speaking or displaying language skills,
- may have insomnia or sleep problems,
- the child may have poor eating and drinking skills,
- the child often wets the bed at night and has difficulty going to the bathroom and doing toilet,
- there are problems with digestion and constipation,
- early or late puberty occurs, cerebral palsy can affect a child with one arm or two arms, one leg or two legs, or one arm and one leg or both arms and both legs.

Types

According to the physical structure, physical ability, and gross motor function's skills, cerebral palsy can be described from different standpoints (Shankar & Mundkur, 2005; Novac, 2014; CP Now, 2015; The Centre for Children with Special Needs, 2011; Bajraszewski, et al., 2008; World Ceribral Palsy Day,

2015).

Such as:

a. **According to the physical structure:**

- **Diplegia:** In this case the child cannot move or stretch the legs at all or has difficulty in moving the legs.

- **Quadriplegia:** Difficulty in moving both hands and legs.

- Hemiplegia: Usually, the upper part of the body is more affected in this case, especially if the child has more difficulty in moving the hand.

b. **According to physical ability:**

- **Spastic:** A typically 70-80% of the body is damaged, resulting in brain-to-body contact disruption. In this case, the baby's brain is damaged, and the muscles become very tight.

- **Dyskinetic:** 10-20% of the body is damaged, the child has difficulty in moving or resting the body. In this case, the baby's basal ganglia are damaged or immature, resulting in speech problems occurring.

- **Ataxia:** About 1-10% of the body is damaged, causing problems in maintaining the balance of the body and the movement of fine motor. In this case, the brain's cerebellum is damaged.

- **Mixed:** Many children may have a combination of any of the above two or three symptoms.

c. **According to gross motor skills movement:**

- **Level 1: Clumsy Child**

  The child from 6 years of age or earlier can walk independently, can climb stairs, run, jump, slow down, maintain balance, coordinate speed and muscle through the motor movement without any additional assistive devices.

- **Level 2: Walks Independently**

  In this case, the child cannot run and jump freely inside the house and in the open space, he finds it difficult to walk in uneven places, crowded and narrow places.

- **Level 3: Uses Assistive Mobility Devices**

  In this case, special equipment such as a crutch, walking sticks, a wheelchair is required for walking inside the house and in the open space.

- **Level 4: Severely Limited**

  In this case the child's movement is restricted by active special equipment. In most cases, the child has to use a wheelchair, but he can drive it himself.

- **Level 5: No Self Mobility**

  In this case the child is completely unable to perform the gross movements, even though with the help of assistive equipment he cannot sit or stand on his own. He needs help from others to stand or sit.

Identification Methods

- Identification methods can be used to evaluate a child's medical history and development skills,
- If identified as a high-risk premature baby by cranial ultrasound after birth.
- Computer tomography scan CT scan or Magnetic Resonance Imaging MRI scan can detect brain injury or accident (My Child Without Limits, n.d.; CP Now, 2015; Shankar & Mundkur, 2005).

Learning Methods

Cerebral palsy cannot be completely eradicated. However, with proper care or services, a child's learning process may improve

(CP Now, 2015; The Centre for Children with Special Needs, 2011; Novac, 2014; My Child Without Limits, n.d.)

- Assistive mobility aids such as crutches, walker, wheelchair, powered scooter; location aids such as - door openers, lighting equipment, seats, standers, sideliners; Magnifier glass to increase vision, textbooks written in large letters; special phone arrangements can be made to increase hearing.

- Medications can be used to manage a child's insomnia, increase brain function, and control drooling and saliva.

- Physiotherapy can improve the ability to sit or walk.

- Stimulate immobilized brain cells and increase muscle function through neuromuscular electrical.

- Nervous system function can be enhanced through instruments, home education.

- Speech and language therapy.

- Occupational therapy.

- Psychologists can identify a child's psychological complications and eliminate them in the light of appropriate counseling.

Appropriate learning strategies tailored to the needs of a child with cerebral palsy in a timely manner can greatly enhance the child's learning process and development.

References

American Academy of Cerebral Palsy and Developmental Medicine. (n.d.). https://www.aacpdm.org

Bajraszewski, E. et al., (2008). 5th ed. *Cerebral Palsy. An information guide for parents.* The Department of Developmental Medicine. Melbourne: The Royal Children Hospital.

CP NOW, Advancing Neuro Recovery. (2005). *The Cerebral Palsy Toolkit. From Diagnosis to Understanding.* 1st ed. South Carolina, USA.

My Child Without Limits. (n.d.). *Introduction to Cerebral Palsy.* www.inclusivechildcare.org/resource-library/website/my-child-without-limits

The Centre for Children with Special Needs. (2011). Revised, 5th ed. *Cerebral Palsy. Critical Elements of Care.* Washington: Seattle Children Hospital.

Novac, I. (2014). Evidence Based Diagnosis, Health Care and Rehabilitation for Children with Cerebral Palsy. *Journal of Child Neurology, 29(8),* 1141-1156.

Reddihough, D. (2011). Cerebral Palsy in Childhood. *Australian*

*Family Physician. Focus: Disability, 40(4),*192-196.

Shankar, C & Mundkur, N. (2005). Cerebral Palsy- Definition, Classification, Etiology and Early Diagnosis. Symposium on Developmental and Behavioral Disorders. *Indian Journal of Pediatrics. 72,* 865-867.

World Cerebral Palsy Day. (2015). *What is Cerebral Palsy?* https://worldcpday.org

Persons with Disabilities Rights and Protection Act, 2013, Section 12. Department of Law and Secretariat, Ministry of Law, and Judiciary. Government of the People's Republic of Bangladesh Dhaka, Bangladesh.

DOWN SYNDROME

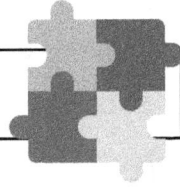

CHAPTER 8

Down Syndrome: Difficulty Due to Extra Copy of 21 Chromosome

Down syndrome is a specific learning disability with developmental delay that is found in childbirth. At first, in 1866 Dr. John Langdon Dawn described the concept 'Down syndrome'. (Down Syndrome Ireland, 2013; National Down Syndrome Society, n.d.). Very keenly he observed some of his patients with special Mongolian physical features that differ from the intellectual disability, so he called them 'Mongol'. Later in 1989 Dr. Jeremy, a French physician, claims in his research that the extra presence of the 21st chromosome during fetal development through cell division in the womb is responsible for Down syndrome. At present, one in every 800-1000 children in the world is born with Down syndrome (Down Syndrome Ireland, 2013). However, in later life, the child may suffer from Alzheimer's disease or dementia (Ibid., 2013).

Causes

- Each baby inherits 23 chromosomes from their parents,

sometimes an extra copy of the 21st chromosome is responsible for the baby's Down syndrome due to an error in cell division during fetal birth in the womb. Although it is not yet known exactly what causes it, researchers agree that it does occur during pregnancy. Generally, mothers more than 35 years of age are at a higher risk of having a child with Down syndrome, however, a woman of any age can have a child with Down syndrome (National Down Syndrome Society, n.d.).

Characteristics

Down syndrome is an inborn developmental difficulty that impairs a child's mental and physical development and persists throughout life. Down syndrome has the following characteristics. (Fidler, 2005; AAPGDS, 2012; Buckley & Bird, 2000; National Down Syndrome Congress, n.d.; Down Syndrome Ireland, 2013; National Down Syndrome Society, n.d.; Disability Rights and Protection Act, 2013):

- The eyes of such a child are almond shaped,
- the nose is flat, the tongue and throat are short,
- the head and hands are relatively small,
- the face is round and flattened, the legs are short even though they have wide feet,
- the muscles of the body are weak,

- the joints of the body are very flexible,
- metabolism is a problem with age, so weight gain is increasing,
- the average height is low,
- generally, low weight at birth.

Characteristically every Down syndrome child is different. Some have less of the above features, and some have more of the features.

Symptoms

(Fidler, 2005; Down Syndrome Ireland, 2013; National Down Syndrome Society, n.d.; Disability Rights and protection Act, 2013):

- Children with Down syndrome usually very slowly achieve the developmental stages (such as sitting, walking, talking).
- There are also weaknesses in learning to speak, difficulty in using proper words and language.
- Visual memory is stronger than auditory memory.
- Children are very good at reading.
- The gross and fine motor skills of the child are impaired.
- Usually up to 10-20% of children with Down syndrome have learning difficulties, such as autism, inattention or

excessive restlessness, ADHD.

- Generally, children with Down syndrome may have some specific health risks, such as visual and auditory impairment, heart abnormalities, breathing difficulties, gastric problems, leukemia, ear and lung problems and others.
- They have difficulty understanding socialization.
- They are usually very friendly with children and adults.

Types

Basically, there are three types of Down syndrome (Down Syndrome Ireland, 2013):

a. **Trisomy 21**

This is the case with 97% of babies with Down syndrome. The extra presence of the 21st chromosome is responsible for this. This happens during pregnancy so that each cell does not make one pair but three.

b. **Translocation**

In 2% of cases Down syndrome can also occur when part of chromosome 21 becomes attached onto another chromosome, before or at conception.

Children with translocation Down syndrome have the usual two copies of chromosome 21 but they also have additional material from chromosome 21 attached to the translocated chromosome.

c. **Mosaic**

1% of people with Down syndrome have a mosaic pattern. They have a mixture of cells, some with an extra chromosome 21 and some normal cells. This mosaic of cells is caused by abnormal cell division after fertilization. some of these babies may present with less of the physical characteristics typically associated with Down Syndrome.

Identification Methods

Down syndrome can usually be detected by ultrasound system during pregnancy and by MRI and computer tomography after birth. Moreover, Down syndrome can be easily recognized by identifying certain physical features (National Down Syndrome Society, n.d.).

Learning Methods

There is no cure for Down Syndrome, but some learning

strategies (Fidler, 2005; Buckley & Bird, 2000; Macintyre, 2002; National Down Syndrome Society, n.d.; Developmental Journal for Down Syndrome, 2008), along with the development of health problems through medication, play a role in the child's psycho-physical development.

- Specific learning profile,
- speech and language therapy,
- occupational therapy,
- sports and technology based specialized education,
- neuro feedback and neuro modulation therapy.

It is possible to make the life of a child with Down syndrome enjoyable by applying appropriate learning techniques.

References

All Parliamentary Group on Down Syndrome (AAPGDS). (2012). Down syndrome: good practice guidelines for education. United Kingdom.

Buckley, S. J. & Bird. G. (2000). Education for individuals with Down syndrome - an overview. *Down Syndrome Education International.* Portsmouth, United Kingdom.

Down Syndrome Ireland. (2013). *Student Information Booklet.* National Leadership Local Support, Ireland.

Early Support Information for Parents-Down Syndrome. (2008). *The Early Support Developmental Journals: Developmental Journal for Down Syndrome.* Department of Education. https://www.education.gov.uk

Fidler, D. (2005). The emerging Down syndrome behavioral phenotype in early childhood. Implication for Practice. *Infants & Young Children, 18(2),* 86-103.

Macintyre, C. (2002). *Play for Children with Special Needs.* London: David Fulton Publishers.

National Down Syndrome Congress. (n.d.). *Down Syndrome: An expectant parents' guide.* Gorgia: National Center. www.ndsccenter.org

National Down Syndrome Society. (n.d.). *Education, Research, Advocacy.* New York, USA. www.ndss.org/about

Persons with Disabilities Rights and Protection Act, 2013, Section 13. Department of Law and Secretariat, Ministry of Law, and Judiciary. Government of the People's Republic of Bangladesh Dhaka, Bangladesh.

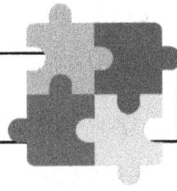

EXAMPLES

CHAPTER 9: Examples

1. Mina is six and a half years old. She was born prematurely (32 weeks) because her mother fell in the bathroom when she was 8 months pregnant and had to have an emergency cesarean section. Mina suffered a brain injury at the time. She cannot walk or talk, she can sit in a wheelchair and move it with her hands, he cannot chew and suck food. At the age of three and a half months, her mother noticed that her physical movements were very poor. She doesn't respond when called by name and can't lift his neck. At 14 months old, she learns to sit, can't blow, but she can hear. She likes to play alone with the key (space needed) ring and the lids of the cooking pots. She is not interested in communicating with peers. She sleeps little at night and often cries and screams in a hoarse voice.

2. Joba is 11 years old. Her Psychophysical development has been the right time. But it was difficult for her to

calculate anything. She can count from 1 to 20 but does not understand the concepts and symbols of addition, subtraction, division, and multiplication and the difference among them. She can't tell the time by looking at the clock. The concept of time, distance, and density is obscure to her. Yet she has normal intelligence.

3. Kalam is 10 years old. His mother had a severe seizure at the time of his birth. He weighed less than two kilograms at birth. He was born with severe jaundice. After 12 days he has a stroke and from one month he learns to suckle. From the age of three months, he often has seizures. At the age of six, he learns to climb stairs without the help of others. Now he can express his thoughts by uttering very limited words. However, he is very friendly.

4. Pritam is 7 years old. At the time of Pritam's birth, his mother was 38 years old. During her mother's pregnancy, doctors identified Pritam as a high-risk child. Ultrasound and computer tomography and other tests are then performed to confirm that there is an additional presence of 21st chromosome in Pritam. He attains developmental stages (walking, talking) much later in life at about five years of age. He looked like a Mongolian,

hands quite short with big eyes. However, he is very friendly with his peers and adults. He could not adapt to the mainstream school curriculum because he was a very slow learner. Now, he has been admitted to a special school.

5. Jarna is 6 years old. She is a full-term child. She did not have any complications at birth. She achieves developmental steps in a timely manner, but her mother notices when she is three years old that she talks too much, does not play and interact with her peers, prefers to be alone, and hides under a bed or behind the door if a guest comes home. She thought Jarna would be fine if she went to school. Regardless, even after being admitted to the school, it was seen that Jarna did not interact with his peers, repeatedly asked the same question to the teacher, tweaking, pinching, and biting his classmates. She is very stubborn. And her emotions are very low, even if she is away from her parents, she does not express her emotions towards them. However, she does not have an intellectual disability.

6. Zahid is 6 years old. He is a premature baby. His mother was diagnosed with diabetes when she was nine weeks

pregnant. Zahid gained weight at his mother's womb because his mother had uncontrolled diabetes, and he was born after 34 weeks. He was born with severe jaundice. He learns to lift his neck at the age of seven months, he learns to sit at the age of 10 months, often he wakes up suddenly at high and cries, and at eighteen months he learns to walk without crawling but still has difficulty balancing his legs. He has difficulty in climbing the stairs on his own. Moreover, he cannot ask for anything by pointing a finger, blowing the flute, or sucking something, he cannot wave his hands. And when excited, he shouts in a hoarse voice, biting his own hand. He often stumbles upon things or people. He cannot understand different stages of cognitive development stages, such as washing hands before and after eating, eating with hands or spoon, going to the toilet, and washing hands in the toilet. He finds it difficult to fasten shoes, eat with a fork, hand write with a pencil, etc. Often, he does not recognize familiar people or places and forgets where things are. He first spoke at the age of three, and now he can say about 100 words. He can't ride a bicycle. He has difficulty catching and throwing the ball. He is naturally very emotional and more friendly with adults than his peers.

7. Rakib is seven years old. At birth he has problems with hypothyroidism, which slows down his learning. He learns to lift his neck at six months, sit at ten months, crawl at 14 months, and walk at 23 months. He learns to bubble too late. So, at first, he learned to say "A" at the age of 26 months, but now he can communicate using the right words. At the age of three, his cognitive development was the equivalent of a 6-month-old child, the equivalent of a 2-year-old at 5 years of age, and now he has the equivalent of a 3-year-old. However, he is good at social interactions with peers and adults. He can read and write some alphabets now, but it takes extra time to practice lessons in the classroom.

8. Riyadh is now four and a half years old. When he was 6 months old, his problems began to take hold, as if he had not responded to the jingle. He learns to lift his neck late, to sit, to call, to crawl, and to walk late. He does not respond when called by name. He can't point fingers at anything, he doesn't participate in imaginative or creative games with his peers, he doesn't interact with his peers, he prefers to be alone in his own world. He can't blow the flute or the bubbles, he doesn't know how to get dressed or go to the toilet, he suddenly smiles and

suddenly cries. He sleeps very little at night and suddenly starts crying, which lasts for a certain period of time. He often shouts in a hoarse voice and cannot speak any meaningful language, speaking in unknown incomprehensible language. Repeatedly opens and closes the door, switches on or off the fan, or light repeatedly. Repeatedly touching the tongue with the hand in the mouth, walking with both hands like the wings of a bird, he bites the other, clapping when excited or biting his own hand. She often has seizures. He also has intellectual disability. At the age of four, he was admitted to a special school.

9. Ratan is 9 years old. He was deprived of oxygen at birth because his mother's labor pains lasted for 36 hours, and Ratan fell into a dry position. He achieved sitting, walking, and other developmental stages at the right time, but he has speech delay. Ever since he went to school at the age of four, his reading problems have become apparent. Ratan has difficulty learning the alphabet and having difficulty identifying and pronouncing singular and collective sounds, he finds it difficult to relate and combine words with sounds and letters. He finds it difficult to spell words and loses letters

or spells while pronouncing words. For example, P is pronounced as Q. He could not understand the difference between the two letters in words. As such, he pronounces. He has difficulty deciphering and copying anything from the board following verbal instructions. He has difficulty reciting rhymes and cannot understand the rhythm in the rhymes. Moreover, he is very inattentive and restless. He has low self-esteem and memory, but he has normal intelligence.

10. Moti is seven and a half years old. Although he has normal intelligence, his handwriting skills are very weak. His handwriting is very obscure, and he misspells words. Such as, write me as mi, you as u, and others. He cannot write with a pencil or a pen. He finds it difficult to write with the movement of the finger and with the balance and coordination of the wrists, arms, and other fingers. He cannot write neatly using lines and margins. He often adds obscure or unknown words to the text. He writes the letters upside down, and the shape and structure of the letters is not correct, like writing 7k upside down, writing 6 as 9. He can't write with space between letters and words. For example, he writes "My name Mati" as *mynamismati*. He writes very slowly.

Answer Examples:

1. Autism and cerebral palsy.
2. Dyscalculia.
3. Cerebral Palsy.
4. Down Syndrome.
5. Autism: Asperger's Syndrome.
6. Dyspraxia.
7. Developmental Delay.
8. Classical Autism.
9. Dyslexia
10. Dysgraphia.

About the Author

SYEDA Khanom

was born in 1981, in Hetimgonj, a suburb of Sylhet District, Bangladesh. Her father was a freedom fighter, and her mother was a housewife. She obtained her bachelor's degree in social work from Shahjalal University of Science and Technology, Sylhet, Bangladesh. Then she moved to London and finished her Master's of Arts in Special and Inclusive Education at the University of Roehampton, London.

She also obtained an MBA in Human Resource Management under the program of York University in London. Recently, in 2023, she completed her Doctor of Philosophy in Education from Selinus University, Italy. At present, she is pursuing a Post Doctoral in Naturopathic Medicine at Kingdom College of Natural Health, USA.

Syeda Khanom has gained teaching experience in three continents of the world (Europe, Asia, and North America). In her entire career she served as a Community Language Teacher in

London, Teacher-Trainer in Bangladesh, and has been working as a substitute teacher in the Metro-Detroit area of Michigan. Currently, she lives in Warren, Michigan, USA. This book is the English version of her Bengali book, "Bishes Shishu: Bishes Chahida-1".

She developed a website www.specialsneeds.com to operate certificate courses to train teachers, parents and others about Special needs.